LIKE A BUCKET LIST, ONLY WAY BETTER

Created by **Lucid Light Journals**:

At Lucid Light Journals, we bring you an abundance of beautifully designed journals & notebooks to bring a ray of light into your or a loved one's life. Search for us in Amazon.

What You'll Find:

★Gratitude & inspirational quote notebooks
★ Health, IF & fitness diaries
★ Wellness journals
★Dream journals
★ Food & cocktail recipe notebooks
★Sketch & comic notebooks, and more...

Music Lover or know one? Visit YourGuitarBrain shop featuring songwriter lyric notebooks, guitar TAB & chord notebooks, music theory books, & music t-shirts which make the perfect gift: **www.yourguitarbrain.com/shop**

Lucid Light
JOURNALS

Journals to inspire & empower

A Gift From:

_____

_____

This Journal
Belongs To:

_____

F*ck It list
[fuk-it-list]

noun:
A list of the things a person (who realises, life is too short, f*ck it, let's go for it) is determined to do or achieve, by hell or high-water, before they bite the dust, meet their maker, shake hands with Elvis, shuffle off this mortal coil, go push up daisies. Go team you!

Tree of Life:

Represents many things across many cultures & philosophies. It's here in this journal to symbolise your life together & you're kick-ass union.

Harmony: you have a lifetime of adventures & laughter ahead of you.

Growth: go live your dreams & build special plans for the future so that you continue to learn and grow together.

Rebirth: life is in a constant cycle; new beginnings & a fresh start are there for the taking. So, get writing down the things you both want to do before you shuffle off this mortal coil and go live the life together you imagined...

YOU Make Us Possible & For That, We Say a Massive Thank-You

You Can Make a Huge Difference:
If You Enjoy Your Journal, Please
Consider Supporting Us & Leave An
Honest Review On Amazon

You Rock!

Shocking, but true...

Did you know most people who write their ideas down in a bucket list only follow through on a few of them?

Our solution is to use a *F*ck It List* instead. Because when you realise life is too short and put pen to paper, you're more likely to say **f*ck it, let's go for it!**

Setting goals with this determined intention will focus your attention and get the fires burning deep inside you.

So, write down your goals, dreams and aspirations in this journal and give your life more meaning, hope & pizazz.

IMPORTANT: Both mildly and wildly unrealistic dreams are also welcome in your *F*ck It List*. As long as it makes you smile and feel excited, write it down.

F*ck it, what you got to lose?

8 Motivating Quotes To Inspire You To Be Fearless & Go Do Life

"Every experience is a success." –
Louise Hay

Twenty years from now, you will be more disappointed by the things you didn't do than by the things you did." –
Mark Twain

"Always choose the future over the past. What do we do now?." – **Brian Tracy**

"If you light a lamp for somebody, it will also brighten your path."
Guatama Buddha

"Don't die with your music still inside you" - **Unknown**

"Stop acting as if life is a rehearsal. Live this day as if it were your last. The past is over and gone." - **Wayne Dyer**

"Remember, it's Ok to get what you want from life." - **Stuart Wilde**

"It always seems impossible until it's done." – **Nelson Mandela**

60 Epic F*ck It List Ideas

1. Explore the historic sites in Petra, Jordan
2. Visit the ancient Mayan city Chichén Itzá, Mexico
3. Stay in an overwater bungalow somewhere like the Maldives or Fiji
4. Go on a cruise through the Norwegian Fjords
5. Hike the Inca Trail to Machu Picchu, Peru
6. Hang out with orangutangs in Borneo
7. Volunteer in an Elephant Sanctuary in Thailand
8. Drive along the Pacific Coast Highway in the USA
9. Visit the preserved ruins in Pompeii, Italy
10. Admire Giant's Causeway in Northern Ireland

HOBBIES

1. Learn to play an instrument
2. Learn to ride a motorcycle
3. Invest in lessons for a current hobby
4. Take up snowboarding
5. Hike to the top of a mountain
6. Learn how to Salsa dance
7. Learn 3 magic tricks to do at your next party
8. Try sailing
9. Learn how to play chess
10. Have a bash at wood carving

60 Epic F*ck It List Ideas

ENTERTAINMENT

1. Watch 10 classic "must-see" movies
2. Go to a drive-in theatre
3. See a play in the West End and/or Broadway
4. Throw a fancy dress party this Halloween
5. Visit a museum
6. Read 10 "must-read" books
7. Go to a live concert
8. Join a local theatre group
9. See the Cirque du Soleil
10. See a live comedian you find hilarious

FOOD

1. Go on a cooking course
2. Buy a foraging book and go explore the undergrowth (loin cloth optional)
3. Make sushi from scratch
4. Bake a cake that doesn't look like a cake
5. Cook something new once a week
6. Brew your own beer or cider
7. Cook a meal over an open fire
8. Make your own pasta
9. Go wine tasting in Provence, France
10. Pick a country, make a dish from there

60 Epic F*ck It List Ideas

GIVING BACK

1. Give blood
2. Adopt an endangered species
3. Cut down on wasteful single-use plastics
4. Eat less meat - start with 2 meat-free days a week
5. Set up a small monthly donation to a charity
6. Wish 3 people "love & peace" silently in your mind every day
7. Next time you see some litter, pick it up, bin it
8. Rescue your next dog or cat
9. Tell a key worker how grateful you are for their hard work (notice how much it means to them)
10. Give phone support to lonely older folks

SELF-LOVE

1. Book a massage
2. Meditate for 10 minutes every day
3. Walk in nature on your own
4. Visit a holy site such as Lourdes to drink in the positive vibes
5. Hug a tree to energy exchange
6. Start jogging. Start small; try a couch to 5k
7. Take up yoga
8. Go on a solo trip to a wellness retreat
9. Start a gratitude journal to remind yourself why you are blessed
10. Don't watch TV for an entire day to quiet the mind

Quick Entry F*ck It List

let's get making happy memories

F*ck It
List

☐

☐

☐

☐

☐

☐

☐

☐

☐

☐

☐

☐

☐

☐

☐

☐

F*ck It List

DONE, IN THE BAG, SMASHED IT

☐

☐

☐

☐

☐

☐

☐

☐

☐

☐

☐

☐

☐

☐

☐

☐

☐

F*ck It List

DONE, IN THE BAG,
SMASHED IT

☐

☐

☐

☐

☐

☐

☐

☐

☐

☐

☐

☐

☐

☐

☐

☐

☐

F*ck It List

☐

☐

☐

☐

☐

☐

☐

☐

☐

☐

☐

☐

☐

☐

☐

☐

☐

TRAVEL
F*ck It List

PLACES TO TRAVEL
(tick when been)

_____ ☐	_____ ☐
_____ ☐	_____ ☐
_____ ☐	_____ ☐
_____ ☐	_____ ☐
_____ ☐	_____ ☐
_____ ☐	_____ ☐
_____ ☐	_____ ☐
_____ ☐	_____ ☐
_____ ☐	_____ ☐
_____ ☐	_____ ☐
_____ ☐	_____ ☐
_____ ☐	_____ ☐
_____ ☐	_____ ☐
_____ ☐	_____ ☐
_____ ☐	_____ ☐
_____ ☐	_____ ☐
_____ ☐	_____ ☐
_____ ☐	_____ ☐
_____ ☐	_____ ☐
_____ ☐	_____ ☐
_____ ☐	_____ ☐

TRAVEL
F*ck It List

PLACES TO TRAVEL
(tick when been)

	☐
	☐
	☐
	☐
	☐
	☐
	☐
	☐
	☐
	☐
	☐
	☐
	☐
	☐
	☐
	☐
	☐
	☐
	☐
	☐

TRAVEL
F*ck It List

PLACES TO TRAVEL
(tick when been)

_____ ☐	_____ ☐
_____ ☐	_____ ☐
_____ ☐	_____ ☐
_____ ☐	_____ ☐
_____ ☐	_____ ☐
_____ ☐	_____ ☐
_____ ☐	_____ ☐
_____ ☐	_____ ☐
_____ ☐	_____ ☐
_____ ☐	_____ ☐
_____ ☐	_____ ☐
_____ ☐	_____ ☐
_____ ☐	_____ ☐
_____ ☐	_____ ☐
_____ ☐	_____ ☐
_____ ☐	_____ ☐
_____ ☐	_____ ☐
_____ ☐	_____ ☐
_____ ☐	_____ ☐

TRAVEL
F*ck It List

PLACES TO TRAVEL
(tick when been)

_____ ☐

_____ ☐

_____ ☐

_____ ☐

_____ ☐

_____ ☐

_____ ☐

_____ ☐

_____ ☐

_____ ☐

_____ ☐

_____ ☐

_____ ☐

_____ ☐

_____ ☐

_____ ☐

_____ ☐

_____ ☐

_____ ☐

_____ ☐

_____ ☐

_____ ☐

_____ ☐

_____ ☐

_____ ☐

_____ ☐

_____ ☐

_____ ☐

_____ ☐

_____ ☐

_____ ☐

_____ ☐

_____ ☐

_____ ☐

_____ ☐

_____ ☐

_____ ☐

_____ ☐

_____ ☐

_____ ☐

Full Page F*ck It List Planner

let's get making happy memories

F*ck It list   EXAMPLE

IDEA / DREAM / ASPIRATION

Volunteer at a local rescue or wildlife
shelter

STEPS TO MAKE THIS HAPPEN

Look up local animal shelters/centres online

Decide which animals to help (any and all!!)

SMASHED IT!

WHEN: 5th July this year

WHERE: Local wildlife centre (once per wk)

WHO WITH: Best friend

IN THREE WORDS: Rewarding, humbling, upliftin.

THE STORY:
We do a range of tasks from feeding
hedgehogs (the babies are adorable!) to
gardening in the nature reserve.
I'm helping pay back the environment &
Mother Nature for making it possible to be
alive. Awesome feeling. Met some great
people doing this too.

life is a gift - go live it in love, light & joy

F*ck It list

Date: _____

IDEA / DREAM / ASPIRATION

_____

_____

STEPS TO MAKE THIS HAPPEN

_____

_____

_____

—•— SMASHED IT! —•—

WHEN: _____

WHERE: _____

WHO WITH: _____

IN THREE WORDS: _____

THE STORY:

_____

_____

_____

_____

_____

_____

_____

life is a gift - go live it in love, light & joy

F*ck It list

IDEA / DREAM / ASPIRATION

_____

_____

STEPS TO MAKE THIS HAPPEN

_____

_____

_____

— • — SMASHED IT! — • —

WHEN: _____

WHERE: _____

WHO WITH: _____

IN THREE WORDS: _____

THE STORY:

_____

_____

_____

_____

_____

_____

_____

_____

life is a gift - go live it in love, light & joy

F*ck It list

Date: _____

IDEA / DREAM / ASPIRATION

_____

_____

STEPS TO MAKE THIS HAPPEN

_____

_____

_____

——•— SMASHED IT! —•——

WHEN: _____

WHERE: _____

WHO WITH: _____

IN THREE WORDS: _____

THE STORY:

_____
_____
_____
_____
_____
_____
_____

life is a gift - go live it in love, light & joy

F*ck It list

Date: _____

IDEA / DREAM / ASPIRATION

_____

_____

STEPS TO MAKE THIS HAPPEN

_____

_____

_____

— •·— SMASHED IT! —·• —

WHEN: _____

WHERE: _____

WHO WITH: _____

IN THREE WORDS: _____

THE STORY:

_____

_____

_____

_____

_____

_____

_____

_____

life is a gift - go live it in love, light & joy

F*ck It list

Date: _____

IDEA / DREAM / ASPIRATION

_____

_____

STEPS TO MAKE THIS HAPPEN

_____

_____

_____

—•— SMASHED IT! —•—

WHEN: _____

WHERE: _____

WHO WITH: _____

IN THREE WORDS: _____

THE STORY:

_____

_____

_____

_____

_____

_____

_____

_____

life is a gift - go live it in love, light & joy

F*ck It List

Date: _____

IDEA / DREAM / ASPIRATION

_____

_____

STEPS TO MAKE THIS HAPPEN

_____

_____

_____

—— •—• —— **SMASHED IT!** —— •—• ——

WHEN: _____

WHERE: _____

WHO WITH: _____

IN THREE WORDS: _____

THE STORY:

_____

_____

_____

_____

_____

_____

_____

_____

life is a gift - go live it in love, light & joy

F*ck It list

Date: _____

IDEA / DREAM / ASPIRATION

_____

_____

STEPS TO MAKE THIS HAPPEN

_____

_____

_____

—•—   **SMASHED IT!**   —•—

WHEN: _____

WHERE: _____

WHO WITH: _____

IN THREE WORDS: _____

THE STORY:

_____

_____

_____

_____

_____

_____

_____

_____

life is a gift - go live it in love, light & joy

F*ck It list

Date: _____

IDEA / DREAM / ASPIRATION

_____

_____

STEPS TO MAKE THIS HAPPEN

_____

_____

_____

—•— SMASHED IT! —•—

WHEN: _____

WHERE: _____

WHO WITH: _____

IN THREE WORDS: _____

THE STORY:

_____

_____

_____

_____

_____

_____

_____

life is a gift - go live it in love, light & joy

F*ck It list

Date: _____

IDEA / DREAM / ASPIRATION

_____

_____

STEPS TO MAKE THIS HAPPEN

_____

_____

_____

————•— SMASHED IT! —•————

WHEN: _____

WHERE: _____

WHO WITH: _____

IN THREE WORDS: _____

THE STORY:

_____

_____

_____

_____

_____

_____

_____

_____

life is a gift - go live it in love, light & joy

F*ck It list

Date: _____

IDEA / DREAM / ASPIRATION

_____

_____

STEPS TO MAKE THIS HAPPEN

_____

_____

_____

———•— SMASHED IT! —•———

WHEN: _____

WHERE: _____

WHO WITH: _____

IN THREE WORDS: _____

THE STORY:

_____

_____

_____

_____

_____

_____

_____

_____

life is a gift - go live it in love, light & joy

F*ck It list

Date: _____

IDEA / DREAM / ASPIRATION

_____

_____

STEPS TO MAKE THIS HAPPEN

_____

_____

_____

—•— **SMASHED IT!** —•—

WHEN: _____

WHERE: _____

WHO WITH: _____

IN THREE WORDS: _____

THE STORY:

_____

_____

_____

_____

_____

_____

_____

_____

life is a gift - go live it in love, light & joy

F*ck It List

Date: _____

IDEA / DREAM / ASPIRATION

_____

_____

STEPS TO MAKE THIS HAPPEN

_____

_____

_____

———•— SMASHED IT! —•———

WHEN: _____

WHERE: _____

WHO WITH: _____

IN THREE WORDS: _____

THE STORY:

_____

_____

_____

_____

_____

_____

_____

_____

life is a gift - go live it in love, light & joy

F*ck It list

Date: _____

IDEA / DREAM / ASPIRATION

_____

_____

STEPS TO MAKE THIS HAPPEN

_____

_____

_____

——•— SMASHED IT! —•——

WHEN: _____

WHERE: _____

WHO WITH: _____

IN THREE WORDS: _____

THE STORY:

_____

_____

_____

_____

_____

_____

_____

life is a gift - go live it in love, light & joy

F*ck It list

Date: _____

IDEA / DREAM / ASPIRATION

_____

_____

STEPS TO MAKE THIS HAPPEN

_____

_____

_____

——•— SMASHED IT! —•——

WHEN: _____

WHERE: _____

WHO WITH: _____

IN THREE WORDS: _____

THE STORY:

_____

_____

_____

_____

_____

_____

_____

life is a gift - go live it in love, light & joy

F*ck It list

Date: _____

IDEA / DREAM / ASPIRATION

_____

_____

STEPS TO MAKE THIS HAPPEN

_____

_____

_____

———•◆•——— SMASHED IT! ———•◆•———

WHEN: _____

WHERE: _____

WHO WITH: _____

IN THREE WORDS: _____

THE STORY:

_____
_____
_____
_____
_____
_____
_____
_____

life is a gift - go live it in love, light & joy

F*ck It List

Date: _____

IDEA / DREAM / ASPIRATION

_____

_____

STEPS TO MAKE THIS HAPPEN

_____

_____

_____

SMASHED IT!

WHEN: _____

WHERE: _____

WHO WITH: _____

IN THREE WORDS: _____

THE STORY:

_____

_____

_____

_____

_____

_____

_____

_____

life is a gift - go live it in love, light & joy

F*ck It list

Date: _____

IDEA / DREAM / ASPIRATION

_____

_____

STEPS TO MAKE THIS HAPPEN

_____

_____

_____

SMASHED IT!

WHEN: _____

WHERE: _____

WHO WITH: _____

IN THREE WORDS: _____

THE STORY:

_____

_____

_____

_____

_____

_____

_____

life is a gift - go live it in love, light & joy

F*ck It list

Date: _____

IDEA / DREAM / ASPIRATION

_____

_____

STEPS TO MAKE THIS HAPPEN

_____

_____

_____

—•— SMASHED IT! —•—

WHEN: _____

WHERE: _____

WHO WITH: _____

IN THREE WORDS: _____

THE STORY:

_____

_____

_____

_____

_____

_____

_____

life is a gift - go live it in love, light & joy

F*ck It list

Date: _____

IDEA / DREAM / ASPIRATION

_____

_____

STEPS TO MAKE THIS HAPPEN

_____

_____

_____

—•— **SMASHED IT!** —•—

WHEN: _____

WHERE: _____

WHO WITH: _____

IN THREE WORDS: _____

THE STORY:

_____

_____

_____

_____

_____

_____

_____

life is a gift - go live it in love, light & joy

F*ck It list

Date: _____

IDEA / DREAM / ASPIRATION

_____

_____

STEPS TO MAKE THIS HAPPEN

_____

_____

_____

——•◆•—— SMASHED IT! ——•◆•——

WHEN: _____

WHERE: _____

WHO WITH: _____

IN THREE WORDS: _____

THE STORY:

_____

_____

_____

_____

_____

_____

_____

life is a gift - go live it in love, light & joy

F*ck It list

Date: _____

IDEA / DREAM / ASPIRATION

_____

_____

STEPS TO MAKE THIS HAPPEN

_____

_____

_____

—•— SMASHED IT! —•—

WHEN: _____

WHERE: _____

WHO WITH: _____

IN THREE WORDS: _____

THE STORY:

_____
_____
_____
_____
_____
_____
_____
_____

life is a gift - go live it in love, light & joy

F*ck It List

Date: _____

IDEA / DREAM / ASPIRATION

_____

_____

STEPS TO MAKE THIS HAPPEN

_____

_____

_____

— • — SMASHED IT! — • —

WHEN: _____

WHERE: _____

WHO WITH: _____

IN THREE WORDS: _____

THE STORY:

_____

_____

_____

_____

_____

_____

_____

_____

life is a gift - go live it in love, light & joy

F*ck It list

Date: _____

IDEA / DREAM / ASPIRATION

_____

_____

STEPS TO MAKE THIS HAPPEN

_____

_____

_____

—•— SMASHED IT! —•—

WHEN: _____

WHERE: _____

WHO WITH: _____

IN THREE WORDS: _____

THE STORY:

_____

_____

_____

_____

_____

_____

_____

life is a gift - go live it in love, light & joy

F*ck It list

Date: _____

IDEA / DREAM / ASPIRATION

_____

_____

STEPS TO MAKE THIS HAPPEN

_____

_____

_____

—•— SMASHED IT! —•—

WHEN: _____

WHERE: _____

WHO WITH: _____

IN THREE WORDS: _____

THE STORY:

_____

_____

_____

_____

_____

_____

_____

life is a gift - go live it in love, light & joy

F*ck It list

Date: _____

IDEA / DREAM / ASPIRATION

_____

_____

STEPS TO MAKE THIS HAPPEN

_____

_____

_____

——•— SMASHED IT! —•——

WHEN: _____

WHERE: _____

WHO WITH: _____

IN THREE WORDS: _____

THE STORY:

_____

_____

_____

_____

_____

_____

_____

life is a gift - go live it in love, light & joy

F*ck It list

Date: _____

IDEA / DREAM / ASPIRATION

_____

_____

STEPS TO MAKE THIS HAPPEN

_____

_____

_____

—•— **SMASHED IT!** —•—

WHEN: _____

WHERE: _____

WHO WITH: _____

IN THREE WORDS: _____

THE STORY:

_____

_____

_____

_____

_____

_____

_____

life is a gift - go live it in love, light & joy

F*ck It list

Date: _____

IDEA / DREAM / ASPIRATION

_____

_____

STEPS TO MAKE THIS HAPPEN

_____

_____

_____

—•— SMASHED IT! —•—

WHEN: _____

WHERE: _____

WHO WITH: _____

IN THREE WORDS: _____

THE STORY:

_____
_____
_____
_____
_____
_____
_____
_____

life is a gift - go live it in love, light & joy

F*ck It list

Date: _____

IDEA / DREAM / ASPIRATION

_____

_____

STEPS TO MAKE THIS HAPPEN

_____

_____

_____

——•—— SMASHED IT! ——•——

WHEN: _____

WHERE: _____

WHO WITH: _____

IN THREE WORDS: _____

THE STORY:

_____

_____

_____

_____

_____

_____

_____

_____

life is a gift - go live it in love, light & joy

F*ck It list

Date: _____

IDEA / DREAM / ASPIRATION

_____

_____

STEPS TO MAKE THIS HAPPEN

_____

_____

_____

—•— **SMASHED IT!** —•—

WHEN: _____

WHERE: _____

WHO WITH: _____

IN THREE WORDS: _____

THE STORY:

_____

_____

_____

_____

_____

_____

_____

_____

life is a gift - go live it in love, light & joy

F*ck It list

Date: _____

IDEA / DREAM / ASPIRATION

_____

_____

STEPS TO MAKE THIS HAPPEN

_____

_____

_____

—•— SMASHED IT! —•—

WHEN: _____

WHERE: _____

WHO WITH: _____

IN THREE WORDS: _____

THE STORY:

_____

_____

_____

_____

_____

_____

_____

life is a gift - go live it in love, light & joy

F*ck It list

Date: _____

IDEA / DREAM / ASPIRATION

_____

_____

STEPS TO MAKE THIS HAPPEN

_____

_____

_____

———•— SMASHED IT! —•———

WHEN: _____

WHERE: _____

WHO WITH: _____

IN THREE WORDS: _____

THE STORY:

_____

_____

_____

_____

_____

_____

life is a gift - go live it in love, light & joy

F*ck It list

Date: _____

IDEA / DREAM / ASPIRATION

_____

_____

STEPS TO MAKE THIS HAPPEN

_____

_____

_____

SMASHED IT!

WHEN: _____

WHERE: _____

WHO WITH: _____

IN THREE WORDS: _____

THE STORY:

_____

_____

_____

_____

_____

_____

_____

life is a gift - go live it in love, light & joy

F*ck It list

Date: _____

IDEA / DREAM / ASPIRATION

_____

_____

STEPS TO MAKE THIS HAPPEN

_____

_____

_____

——•◆•—— SMASHED IT! ——•◆•——

WHEN: _____

WHERE: _____

WHO WITH: _____

IN THREE WORDS: _____

THE STORY:

_____
_____
_____
_____
_____
_____
_____
_____

life is a gift - go live it in love, light & joy

F*ck It list

Date: _____

IDEA / DREAM / ASPIRATION

_____

_____

STEPS TO MAKE THIS HAPPEN

_____

_____

_____

—•— SMASHED IT! —•—

WHEN: _____

WHERE: _____

WHO WITH: _____

IN THREE WORDS: _____

THE STORY:

_____
_____
_____
_____
_____
_____
_____
_____

life is a gift - go live it in love, light & joy

F*ck It list

Date: _____

IDEA / DREAM / ASPIRATION

_____

_____

STEPS TO MAKE THIS HAPPEN

_____

_____

_____

———•—— SMASHED IT! ——•———

WHEN: _____

WHERE: _____

WHO WITH: _____

IN THREE WORDS: _____

THE STORY:

_____

_____

_____

_____

_____

_____

_____

life is a gift - go live it in love, light & joy

F*ck It list

Date: _____

IDEA / DREAM / ASPIRATION

_____

_____

STEPS TO MAKE THIS HAPPEN

_____

_____

_____

——•— SMASHED IT! —•——

WHEN: _____

WHERE: _____

WHO WITH: _____

IN THREE WORDS: _____

THE STORY:

_____

_____

_____

_____

_____

_____

_____

life is a gift - go live it in love, light & joy

F*ck It list

Date: _____

IDEA / DREAM / ASPIRATION

_____
_____

STEPS TO MAKE THIS HAPPEN

_____
_____
_____

SMASHED IT!

WHEN: _____

WHERE: _____

WHO WITH: _____

IN THREE WORDS: _____

THE STORY:

_____
_____
_____
_____
_____
_____
_____

life is a gift - go live it in love, light & joy

F*ck It list

Date: _____

IDEA / DREAM / ASPIRATION

_____

_____

STEPS TO MAKE THIS HAPPEN

_____

_____

_____

— • — SMASHED IT! — • —

WHEN: _____

WHERE: _____

WHO WITH: _____

IN THREE WORDS: _____

THE STORY:

_____

_____

_____

_____

_____

_____

_____

life is a gift - go live it in love, light & joy

F*ck It list

Date: _____

IDEA / DREAM / ASPIRATION

_____

_____

STEPS TO MAKE THIS HAPPEN

_____

_____

_____

——•·◦·•—— SMASHED IT! ——•·◦·•——

WHEN: _____

WHERE: _____

WHO WITH: _____

IN THREE WORDS: _____

THE STORY:

_____

_____

_____

_____

_____

_____

_____

_____

_____

life is a gift - go live it in love, light & joy

F*ck It list

Date: _____

IDEA / DREAM / ASPIRATION

_____

_____

STEPS TO MAKE THIS HAPPEN

_____

_____

_____

—•— **SMASHED IT!** —•—

WHEN: _____

WHERE: _____

WHO WITH: _____

IN THREE WORDS: _____

THE STORY:

_____

_____

_____

_____

_____

_____

_____

_____

life is a gift - go live it in love, light & joy

F*ck It list

Date: _____

IDEA / DREAM / ASPIRATION

_____

_____

STEPS TO MAKE THIS HAPPEN

_____

_____

_____

—•— **SMASHED IT!** —•—

WHEN: _____

WHERE: _____

WHO WITH: _____

IN THREE WORDS: _____

THE STORY:

_____

_____

_____

_____

_____

_____

_____

_____

life is a gift - go live it in love, light & joy

F*ck It list

Date: _____

IDEA / DREAM / ASPIRATION

_____

_____

STEPS TO MAKE THIS HAPPEN

_____

_____

_____

———•— SMASHED IT! —•———

WHEN: _____

WHERE: _____

WHO WITH: _____

IN THREE WORDS: _____

THE STORY:

_____

_____

_____

_____

_____

_____

_____

_____

life is a gift - go live it in love, light & joy

F*ck It list

Date: _____

IDEA / DREAM / ASPIRATION

_____

_____

STEPS TO MAKE THIS HAPPEN

_____

_____

_____

——• SMASHED IT! •——

WHEN: _____

WHERE: _____

WHO WITH: _____

IN THREE WORDS: _____

THE STORY:

_____

_____

_____

_____

_____

_____

_____

_____

life is a gift - go live it in love, light & joy

F*ck It list

Date: _____

IDEA / DREAM / ASPIRATION

_____

_____

STEPS TO MAKE THIS HAPPEN

_____

_____

_____

SMASHED IT!

WHEN: _____

WHERE: _____

WHO WITH: _____

IN THREE WORDS: _____

THE STORY:

_____

_____

_____

_____

_____

_____

_____

life is a gift - go live it in love, light & joy

F*ck It list

Date: _____

IDEA / DREAM / ASPIRATION

_____

_____

STEPS TO MAKE THIS HAPPEN

_____

_____

_____

— •— SMASHED IT! —•—

WHEN: _____

WHERE: _____

WHO WITH: _____

IN THREE WORDS: _____

THE STORY:

_____
_____
_____
_____
_____
_____
_____
_____
_____

life is a gift - go live it in love, light & joy

F*ck It list

Date: _____

IDEA / DREAM / ASPIRATION

_____

_____

STEPS TO MAKE THIS HAPPEN

_____

_____

_____

—•— SMASHED IT! —•—

WHEN: _____

WHERE: _____

WHO WITH: _____

IN THREE WORDS: _____

THE STORY:

_____

_____

_____

_____

_____

_____

_____

life is a gift – go live it in love, light & joy

F*ck It list

Date: _____

IDEA / DREAM / ASPIRATION

_____

_____

STEPS TO MAKE THIS HAPPEN

_____

_____

_____

—•— SMASHED IT! —•—

WHEN: _____

WHERE: _____

WHO WITH: _____

IN THREE WORDS: _____

THE STORY:

_____

_____

_____

_____

_____

_____

_____

_____

life is a gift - go live it in love, light & joy

F*ck It list

Date: _____

IDEA / DREAM / ASPIRATION

_____

_____

STEPS TO MAKE THIS HAPPEN

_____

_____

_____

—•— SMASHED IT! —•—

WHEN: _____

WHERE: _____

WHO WITH: _____

IN THREE WORDS: _____

THE STORY:

_____

_____

_____

_____

_____

_____

_____

_____

life is a gift - go live it in love, light & joy

F*ck It list

Date: _____

IDEA / DREAM / ASPIRATION

_____

_____

STEPS TO MAKE THIS HAPPEN

_____

_____

_____

——•— SMASHED IT! —•——

WHEN: _____

WHERE: _____

WHO WITH: _____

IN THREE WORDS: _____

THE STORY:

_____

_____

_____

_____

_____

_____

_____

_____

life is a gift - go live it in love, light & joy

F*ck It list

Date: _____

IDEA / DREAM / ASPIRATION

_____

_____

STEPS TO MAKE THIS HAPPEN

_____

_____

_____

——•— SMASHED IT! —•——

WHEN: _____

WHERE: _____

WHO WITH: _____

IN THREE WORDS: _____

THE STORY:

_____

_____

_____

_____

_____

_____

_____

_____

life is a gift - go live it in love, light & joy

F*ck It list

Date: _____

IDEA / DREAM / ASPIRATION

_____

_____

STEPS TO MAKE THIS HAPPEN

_____

_____

_____

———•— SMASHED IT! —•———

WHEN: _____

WHERE: _____

WHO WITH: _____

IN THREE WORDS: _____

THE STORY:

_____
_____
_____
_____
_____
_____
_____
_____
_____

life is a gift - go live it in love, light & joy

F*ck It list

Date: _____

IDEA / DREAM / ASPIRATION

_____

_____

STEPS TO MAKE THIS HAPPEN

_____

_____

_____

— • — **SMASHED IT!** — • —

WHEN: _____

WHERE: _____

WHO WITH: _____

IN THREE WORDS: _____

THE STORY:

_____

_____

_____

_____

_____

_____

_____

life is a gift – go live it in love, light & joy

F*ck It list

Date: _____

IDEA / DREAM / ASPIRATION

_____

_____

STEPS TO MAKE THIS HAPPEN

_____

_____

_____

_____

—•— SMASHED IT! —•—

WHEN: _____

WHERE: _____

WHO WITH: _____

IN THREE WORDS: _____

THE STORY:

_____

_____

_____

_____

_____

_____

_____

life is a gift - go live it in love, light & joy

F*ck It list

Date: _____

IDEA / DREAM / ASPIRATION

_____

_____

STEPS TO MAKE THIS HAPPEN

_____

_____

_____

—•— SMASHED IT! —•—

WHEN: _____

WHERE: _____

WHO WITH: _____

IN THREE WORDS: _____

THE STORY:

_____

_____

_____

_____

_____

_____

life is a gift - go live it in love, light & joy

F*ck It list

Date: _____

IDEA / DREAM / ASPIRATION

_____

_____

STEPS TO MAKE THIS HAPPEN

_____

_____

_____

———•• SMASHED IT! ••———

WHEN: _____

WHERE: _____

WHO WITH: _____

IN THREE WORDS: _____

THE STORY:

_____

_____

_____

_____

_____

_____

_____

life is a gift - go live it in love, light & joy

F*ck It list

Date: _____

IDEA / DREAM / ASPIRATION

_____

_____

STEPS TO MAKE THIS HAPPEN

_____

_____

_____

— • — SMASHED IT! — • —

WHEN: _____

WHERE: _____

WHO WITH: _____

IN THREE WORDS: _____

THE STORY:

_____

_____

_____

_____

_____

_____

_____

life is a gift - go live it in love, light & joy

F*ck It list

Date: _____

IDEA / DREAM / ASPIRATION

_____

_____

STEPS TO MAKE THIS HAPPEN

_____

_____

_____

———•—— SMASHED IT! ——•———

WHEN: _____

WHERE: _____

WHO WITH: _____

IN THREE WORDS: _____

THE STORY:

_____
_____
_____
_____
_____
_____
_____
_____

life is a gift - go live it in love, light & joy

F*ck It list

Date: _____

IDEA / DREAM / ASPIRATION

_____

_____

STEPS TO MAKE THIS HAPPEN

_____

_____

_____

━━•◆•━━ SMASHED IT! ━━•◆•━━

WHEN: _____

WHERE: _____

WHO WITH: _____

IN THREE WORDS: _____

THE STORY:

_____

_____

_____

_____

_____

_____

_____

_____

life is a gift - go live it in love, light & joy

F*ck It list

Date: _____

IDEA / DREAM / ASPIRATION

_____

_____

STEPS TO MAKE THIS HAPPEN

_____

_____

_____

SMASHED IT!

WHEN: _____

WHERE: _____

WHO WITH: _____

IN THREE WORDS: _____

THE STORY:

_____

_____

_____

_____

_____

_____

_____

life is a gift - go live it in love, light & joy

F*ck It list

Date: _____

IDEA / DREAM / ASPIRATION

_____

_____

STEPS TO MAKE THIS HAPPEN

_____

_____

_____

——•— SMASHED IT! —•——

WHEN: _____

WHERE: _____

WHO WITH: _____

IN THREE WORDS: _____

THE STORY:

_____

_____

_____

_____

_____

_____

_____

life is a gift - go live it in love, light & joy

F*ck It list

Date: _____

IDEA / DREAM / ASPIRATION

_____

_____

STEPS TO MAKE THIS HAPPEN

_____

_____

_____

SMASHED IT!

WHEN: _____

WHERE: _____

WHO WITH: _____

IN THREE WORDS: _____

THE STORY:

_____

_____

_____

_____

_____

_____

life is a gift - go live it in love, light & joy

F*ck It list

Date: _____

IDEA / DREAM / ASPIRATION

_____

_____

STEPS TO MAKE THIS HAPPEN

_____

_____

_____

———•— SMASHED IT! —•———

WHEN: _____

WHERE: _____

WHO WITH: _____

IN THREE WORDS: _____

THE STORY:

_____

_____

_____

_____

_____

_____

_____

life is a gift – go live it in love, light & joy

F*ck It list

Date: _____

IDEA / DREAM / ASPIRATION

_____

_____

STEPS TO MAKE THIS HAPPEN

_____

_____

_____

———•—• SMASHED IT! —•—

WHEN: _____

WHERE: _____

WHO WITH: _____

IN THREE WORDS: _____

THE STORY:

_____

_____

_____

_____

_____

_____

_____

life is a gift - go live it in love, light & joy

F*ck It list

Date: _____

IDEA / DREAM / ASPIRATION

_____

_____

STEPS TO MAKE THIS HAPPEN

_____

_____

_____

———•— SMASHED IT! —•———

WHEN: _____

WHERE: _____

WHO WITH: _____

IN THREE WORDS: _____

THE STORY:

_____

_____

_____

_____

_____

_____

_____

life is a gift - go live it in love, light & joy

F*ck It list

Date: _____

IDEA / DREAM / ASPIRATION

_____

_____

STEPS TO MAKE THIS HAPPEN

_____

_____

_____

——•·—— SMASHED IT! ——·•——

WHEN: _____

WHERE: _____

WHO WITH: _____

IN THREE WORDS: _____

THE STORY:

_____

_____

_____

_____

_____

_____

_____

life is a gift - go live it in love, light & joy

F*ck It list

Date: _____

IDEA / DREAM / ASPIRATION

_____

_____

STEPS TO MAKE THIS HAPPEN

_____

_____

_____

SMASHED IT!

WHEN: _____

WHERE: _____

WHO WITH: _____

IN THREE WORDS: _____

THE STORY:

_____

_____

_____

_____

_____

_____

_____

_____

life is a gift - go live it in love, light & joy

F*ck It list

Date: _____

IDEA / DREAM / ASPIRATION

_____

_____

STEPS TO MAKE THIS HAPPEN

_____

_____

_____

SMASHED IT!

WHEN: _____

WHERE: _____

WHO WITH: _____

IN THREE WORDS: _____

THE STORY:

_____

_____

_____

_____

_____

_____

_____

life is a gift - go live it in love, light & joy

F*ck It list

Date: _____

IDEA / DREAM / ASPIRATION

_____

_____

STEPS TO MAKE THIS HAPPEN

_____

_____

_____

— •— SMASHED IT! —• —

WHEN: _____

WHERE: _____

WHO WITH: _____

IN THREE WORDS: _____

THE STORY:

_____

_____

_____

_____

_____

_____

_____

life is a gift – go live it in love, light & joy

F*ck It list

Date: _____

IDEA / DREAM / ASPIRATION

_____

_____

STEPS TO MAKE THIS HAPPEN

_____

_____

_____

SMASHED IT!

WHEN: _____

WHERE: _____

WHO WITH: _____

IN THREE WORDS: _____

THE STORY:

_____
_____
_____
_____
_____
_____
_____
_____

life is a gift - go live it in love, light & joy

F*ck It list

Date: _____

IDEA / DREAM / ASPIRATION

_____

_____

STEPS TO MAKE THIS HAPPEN

_____

_____

_____

— • — **SMASHED IT!** — • —

WHEN: _____

WHERE: _____

WHO WITH: _____

IN THREE WORDS: _____

THE STORY:

_____
_____
_____
_____
_____
_____
_____

life is a gift - go live it in love, light & joy

F*ck It list

Date: _____

IDEA / DREAM / ASPIRATION

_____

_____

STEPS TO MAKE THIS HAPPEN

_____

_____

_____

———•·—— SMASHED IT! ——·•———

WHEN: _____

WHERE: _____

WHO WITH: _____

IN THREE WORDS: _____

THE STORY:

_____

_____

_____

_____

_____

_____

_____

_____

life is a gift - go live it in love, light & joy

F*ck It list

Date: _____

IDEA / DREAM / ASPIRATION

_____

_____

STEPS TO MAKE THIS HAPPEN

_____

_____

_____

SMASHED IT!

WHEN: _____

WHERE: _____

WHO WITH: _____

IN THREE WORDS: _____

THE STORY:

_____

_____

_____

_____

_____

_____

_____

_____

life is a gift - go live it in love, light & joy

F*ck It list

Date: _____

IDEA / DREAM / ASPIRATION

_____

_____

STEPS TO MAKE THIS HAPPEN

_____

_____

_____

SMASHED IT!

WHEN: _____

WHERE: _____

WHO WITH: _____

IN THREE WORDS: _____

THE STORY:

_____

_____

_____

_____

_____

_____

_____

life is a gift - go live it in love, light & joy

F*ck It list

Date: _____

IDEA / DREAM / ASPIRATION

_____

_____

STEPS TO MAKE THIS HAPPEN

_____

_____

_____

—•— SMASHED IT! —•—

WHEN: _____

WHERE: _____

WHO WITH: _____

IN THREE WORDS: _____

THE STORY:

_____

_____

_____

_____

_____

_____

_____

_____

life is a gift – go live it in love, light & joy

F*ck It list

Date: _____

IDEA / DREAM / ASPIRATION

_____

_____

STEPS TO MAKE THIS HAPPEN

_____

_____

_____

SMASHED IT!

WHEN: _____

WHERE: _____

WHO WITH: _____

IN THREE WORDS: _____

THE STORY:

_____
_____
_____
_____
_____
_____
_____
_____
_____

life is a gift - go live it in love, light & joy

F*ck It list

Date: _____

IDEA / DREAM / ASPIRATION

_____

_____

STEPS TO MAKE THIS HAPPEN

_____

_____

_____

— • — SMASHED IT! — • —

WHEN: _____

WHERE: _____

WHO WITH: _____

IN THREE WORDS: _____

THE STORY:

_____

_____

_____

_____

_____

_____

_____

life is a gift - go live it in love, light & joy

F*ck It list

Date: _____

IDEA / DREAM / ASPIRATION

_____

_____

STEPS TO MAKE THIS HAPPEN

_____

_____

_____

—•— **SMASHED IT!** —•—

WHEN: _____

WHERE: _____

WHO WITH: _____

IN THREE WORDS: _____

THE STORY:

_____
_____
_____
_____
_____
_____
_____

life is a gift - go live it in love, light & joy

F*ck It list

Date: _____

IDEA / DREAM / ASPIRATION

_____

_____

STEPS TO MAKE THIS HAPPEN

_____

_____

_____

━━•·━━ SMASHED IT! ━━•·━━

WHEN: _____

WHERE: _____

WHO WITH: _____

IN THREE WORDS: _____

THE STORY:

_____

_____

_____

_____

_____

_____

_____

life is a gift - go live it in love, light & joy

F*ck It list

Date: _____

IDEA / DREAM / ASPIRATION

_____

_____

STEPS TO MAKE THIS HAPPEN

_____

_____

_____

SMASHED IT!

WHEN: _____

WHERE: _____

WHO WITH: _____

IN THREE WORDS: _____

THE STORY:

_____

_____

_____

_____

_____

_____

_____

life is a gift - go live it in love, light & joy

Created by Lucid Light Journals:

At Lucid Light Journals, we bring you an abundance of beautifully designed journals & notebooks to bring a ray of light into your or a loved one's life. Search for us in Amazon.

What You'll Find:

★ Gratitude & inspirational quote notebooks
★ Health, IF & fitness diaries
★ Wellness journals
★ Dream journals
★ Food & cocktail recipe notebooks
★ Sketch & comic notebooks, and more...

Music Lover or know one? Visit YourGuitarBrain shop featuring songwriter lyric notebooks, guitar TAB & chord notebooks, music theory books, & music t-shirts which make the perfect gift:

www.yourguitarbrain.com/shop

Printed in Great Britain
by Amazon